D0682395

The Bournemouth & Poole College

250257622 V

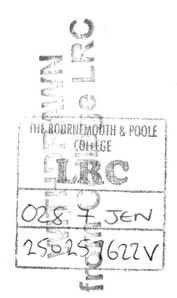

THE BOURNEMOUTH & POOLE
COLLEGE
LRC

028.7 JEN

250257622V

First
Facts®

ALL ABOUT MEDIA

FACT, FICTION AND OPINIONS:

THE DIFFERENCE BETWEEN ADS, BLOGS, NEWS REPORTS AND OTHER MEDIA

BRIEN J JENNINGS

raintree

a Capstone company — publishers for children

Raintree is an imprint of Capstone Global Library Limited, a company incorporated in England and Wales having its registered office at 264 Banbury Road, Oxford, OX2 7DY – Registered company number: 6695582

www.raintree.co.uk
myorders@raintree.co.uk

Text © Capstone Global Library Limited 2018
The moral rights of the proprietor have been asserted.

All rights reserved. No part of this publication may be reproduced in any form or by any means (including photocopying or storing it in any medium by electronic means and whether or not transiently or incidentally to some other use of this publication) without the written permission of the copyright owner, except in accordance with the provisions of the Copyright, Designs and Patents Act 1988 or under the terms of a licence issued by the Copyright Licensing Agency, Saffron House, 6–10 Kirby Street, London EC1N 8TS (www.cla.co.uk). Applications for the copyright owner's written permission should be addressed to the publisher.

ISBN 978 1 4747 5441 5
22 21 20 19 18
10 9 8 7 6 5 4 3 2 1

THE BOURNEMOUTH & POOLE
COLLEGE
LRC

250257622 V

Editorial credits:
Erika L. Shores, editor; Juliette Peters, designer;
Morgan Walters, media researcher; Kathy McColley, production specialist
Printed and bound in India

Photo credits:
Alamy: Agencja Fotograficzna Caro, 5, Hero Images Inc., 15, Jeff Greenberg 6 of 6, 17; Shutterstock: Africa Studio, 11, Akkaradet Bangchun, (tv) 12, Anutr Yossundara, 20, Artur. B, (icons) design element, Charts and Table, Cover, Denis Rozhnovsky, (billboard) 12, Di Studio, (blog) 12, Duplass, left Cover, Mat Hayward, 7, MITstudio, (drink) 12, MK photograp55, 14, Rawpixel.com, 21, Roman Tiraspolsky, 13, Supphachai Salaeman, design element throughout, VGstockstudio, 19, vmalafeevskiy, (fast food) 12, wavebreakmedia, 9

British Library Cataloguing in Publication Data
A full catalogue record for this book is available from the British Library.

Every effort has been made to contact copyright holders of material reproduced in this book. Any omissions will be rectified in subsequent printings if notice is given to the publisher.

All the Internet addresses (URLs) given in this book were valid at the time of going to press. However, due to the dynamic nature of the Internet, some addresses may have changed, or sites may have changed or ceased to exist since publication. While the author and publisher regret any inconvenience this may cause readers, no responsibility for any such changes can be accepted by either the author or the publisher.

Contents

All about media

What do ads, **blogs** and news reports have in common? They are types of media. Books, websites, films, TV programmes and **apps** are media as well. Media sends a message. An **audience** receives the message.

blog diary on the internet; blog is short for weblog
app programme that is downloaded to computers and
mobile devices; app is short for application
audience people who hear, read or see a message

Who is the audience for media messages? You are! So it's up to you to ask a lot of questions. Ask questions to understand the media maker's **purpose**. Why was the message created? Understanding the purpose helps you to work out if the media's message is fact, fiction or opinion.

purpose reason for which something is made or done

Media informs, entertains and **persuades**. Media that informs includes facts. Facts are true. We check facts by finding **evidence**.

If the purpose of media is to entertain, then it may be fiction. Fiction is not true. It is made up.

Sometimes the purpose of media is to persuade. This type of media often includes opinions. An opinion is an idea or feeling about something. An opinion is not the same as a fact. We can't prove opinions are true.

Questions to ask about media:

Who created the media?

Who is the audience for the media?

How does the author try to keep the audience's attention?

Why was the media created?

Does it give important information (inform)?

Does it tell a story, make you laugh, cry or feel a certain way (entertain)?

Does it try to change your mind or convince you of something (persuade)?

evidence information, items and facts that help prove something to be true or false

persuade change a person's mind

9

Ads

Advertisements, also called ads, are made to sell something. They're not fiction, and they're not always an opinion. The main purpose of an ad is to persuade or to get you to buy something. Ads may also try to change your mind about a topic or product.

advertisement notice that calls attention to a product or an event

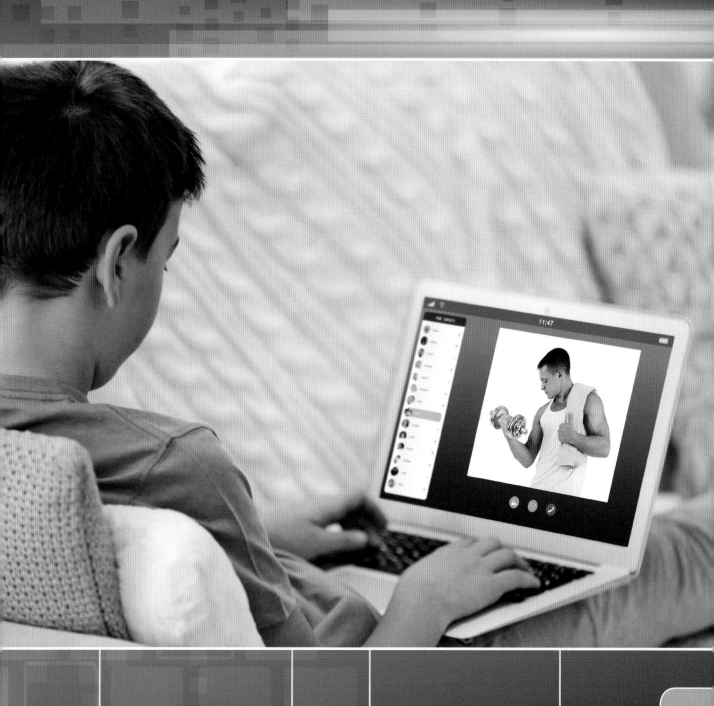

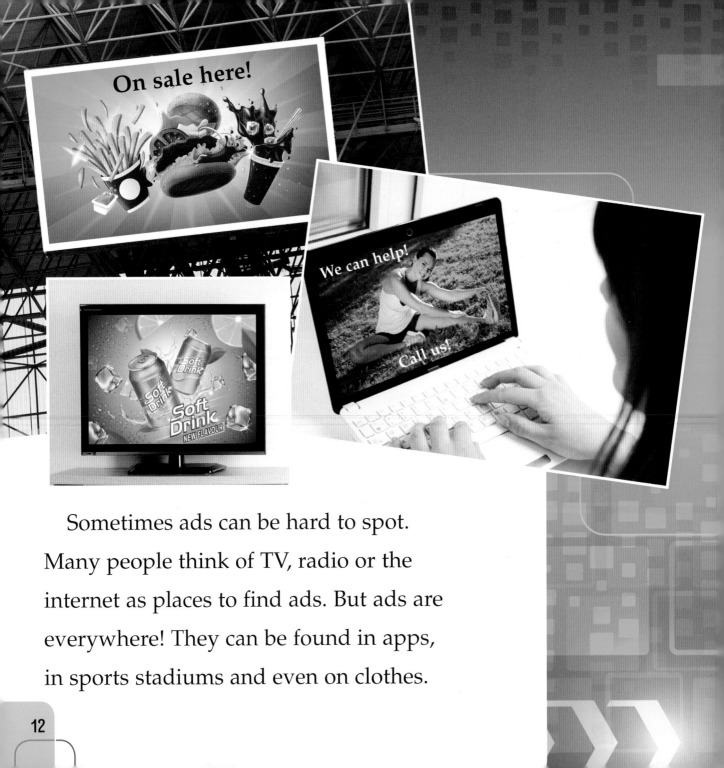

Sometimes ads can be hard to spot. Many people think of TV, radio or the internet as places to find ads. But ads are everywhere! They can be found in apps, in sports stadiums and even on clothes.

Think about it!

Brands or **logos** on cars, clothing or buildings are all advertising.

logo picture or symbol that a company puts on its products

13

Blogs

A blog is a website people use to keep an online diary. People who write or record blogs are called bloggers. Anyone can be a blogger. Some bloggers share real news events. Others share their thoughts and opinions about news events, games, toys or other topics. You must check other sources before trusting that information on a blog is true.

Think about it!

Blog is short for weblog. Blogs can be fun to read or watch. But make sure you pay attention and think carefully about the information a blogger is sharing. Where is the information coming from? Is it fact or opinion?

News reports

News reports give the facts about events in your local area, country and the world. A reporter's job is to provide a true account of news events. The reporter does this by answering six main questions – who, what, why, where, when and how.

You need to think carefully about news reports you read or hear. Sometimes stories that appear to be news reports are really ads. Sometimes news reports won't include all the facts or both sides of a story. Ask yourself whether or not the news report left out information. Did the report only tell one side of the story? Did the news report include the writer's opinions?

FACT Today many people read news reports they see posted on **social media**.

social media websites that allow people to share words, pictures and videos with other people

19

Everything in between

You see and use media every day. People share opinions with friends on social media. People visit websites to watch videos. Media messages are everywhere. Sometimes it can be hard to tell the difference between fact, fiction and opinion. TV programmes and games can be entertaining and have ads. It's easy for bloggers to mix facts and opinions. That's why it's important for you to question what you read, hear or see in the media.

TRY IT! Look at some ads in magazines or online. Imagine something you'd like to sell, such as a new toy. Write an ad for it. Who is your audience? How will you get your audience to pay attention? Will you use pictures? If you video your ad, will you use music?

Glossary

advertisement notice that calls attention to a product or an event

app programme that is downloaded to computers and mobile devices; app is short for application

audience people who hear, read or see a message

blog diary on the internet; blog is short for weblog

evidence information, items and facts that help prove something to be true or false

logo picture or symbol that a company puts on its products

persuade change a person's mind

purpose reason for which something is made or done

social media websites that allow people to share words, pictures and videos with other people

Books

I Can Write Reports (I Can Write), Anita Ganeri (Raintree, 2013)

Learning About Plagiarism (Media Literacy for Kids), Nikki Bruno Clapper (Raintree, 2015)

Let's Think About the Internet and Social Media (Let's Think About), Alex Woolf (Raintree, 2015)

Websites

www.bbc.co.uk/newsround
The BBC newsround website is just one place to stay up-to-date with news events from around the world.

www.dkfindout.com/uk/explore/top-internet-tips-to-stay-safe-online/
Looking at online media can be fun and informative – but make sure you follow these top tips to stay safe.

THE BOURNEMOUTH & POOLE COLLEGE
LRC

Comprehension questions

1. What is the purpose of a news report?

2. If you had your own blog, what would you write about and why?

3. Describe the difference between a fact and an opinion.

Index